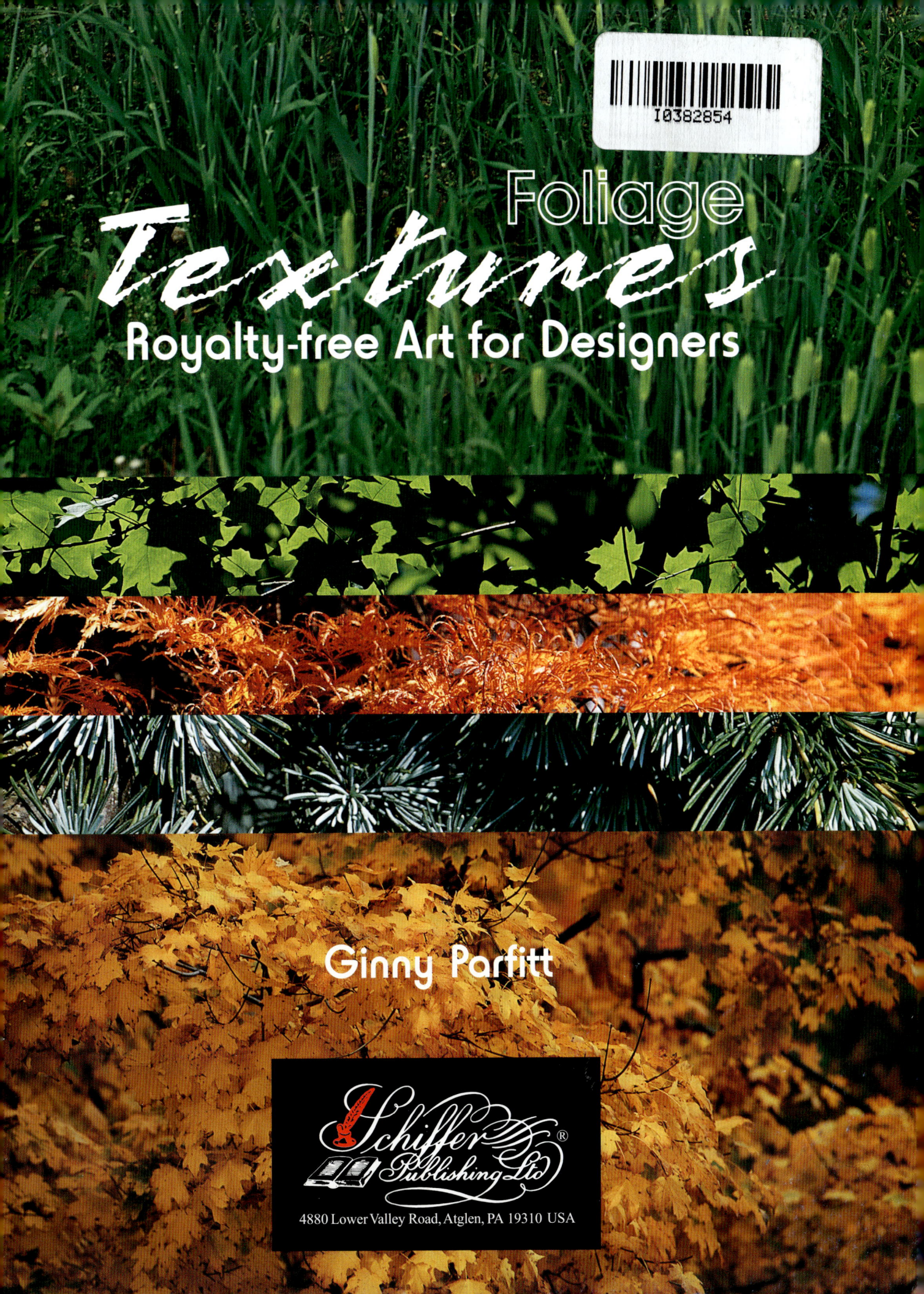
Foliage Textures
Royalty-free Art for Designers

Ginny Parfitt

Schiffer Publishing Ltd
4880 Lower Valley Road, Atglen, PA 19310 USA

Contents

Summer Foliage 3
Autumn Foliage 23
Evergreen Foliage 39
Tropical & Succulent, Ferns & Cacti 48
Grasses & Groundcovers 76
Single, Cluster, & Silhouettes 96

NOTICE OF RIGHTS

These images are copyrighted pursuant to 17 U.S.C. 101 et seq. The purchase of this book and accompanying CD gives you a limited license to use up to five images on the CD for personal or commercial projects, without additional compensation or permission. Any other republication or reproduction of any image in this book or on this CD by any other graphic service, including print, electronic, known, and unknown sources, is strictly prohibited, as is the transmission of files.

Images on the CD are presented at approximately 4" x 6" at 300 dpi. Larger images are available from the publisher at appropriate rates. Use the link on the CD to the Schiffer Publishing website. All contact information can be found there.

Managing Editor: Ginny Parfitt
Cover and Book Design: John Cheek

Copyright © 2005 by Schiffer Publishing
Library of Congress Card Number: 2005928198

All rights reserved. No part of this work may be reproduced or used in any form or by any means—graphic, electronic, or mechanical, including photocopying or information storage and retrieval systems—without written permission from the publisher.

The scanning, uploading and distribution of this book or any part thereof via the Internet or via any other means without the permission of the publisher is illegal and punishable by law. Please purchase only authorized editions and do not participate in or encourage the electronic piracy of copyrighted materials.

"Schiffer," "Schiffer Publishing Ltd. & Design," and the "Design of pen and ink well" are registered trademarks of Schiffer Publishing Ltd.

Type set in Bronx LET/Korinna BT

ISBN: 0-7643-2289-3
Printed in China

Published by Schiffer Publishing Ltd.
4880 Lower Valley Road
Atglen, PA 19310
Phone: (610) 593-1777; Fax: (610) 593-2002
E-mail: Info@schifferbooks.com

For the largest selection of fine reference books on this and related subjects, please visit our web site at **www.schifferbooks.com**
We are always looking for people to write books on new and related subjects. If you have an idea for a book please contact us at the above address.

This book may be purchased from the publisher.
Include $3.95 for shipping.
Please try your bookstore first.
You may write for a free catalog.

In Europe, Schiffer books are distributed by
Bushwood Books
6 Marksbury Ave.
Kew Gardens
Surrey TW9 4JF England
Phone: 44 (0) 20 8392-8585;
Fax: 44 (0) 20 8392-9876
E-mail: info@bushwoodbooks.co.uk
Free postage in the U.K., Europe; air mail at cost.

Summer Foliage

4

Summer Foliage

Summer Foliage

Summer Foliage

Summer Foliage

Summer Foliage

Summer Foliage

Summer Foliage

Summer Foliage

12

Summer Foliage

Summer Foliage

Summer Foliage

Summer Foliage

Summer Foliage

Autumn Foliage

Autumn Foliage

Autumn Foliage

26

Autumn Foliage

Autumn Foliage

Autumn Foliage

Autumn Foliage

Autumn Foliage

Autumn Foliage

Autumn Foliage

Autumn Foliage

Autumn Foliage

Evergreen Foliage

Evergreen Foliage

Evergreen Foliage

42

Evergreen Foliage

Evergreen Foliage

Tropical & Succulent Ferns & Cacti

Tropical & Succulent Foliage, Ferns and Cacti

Tropical & Succulent Foliage, Ferns and Cacti

Tropical & Succulent Foliage, Ferns and Cacti

Grasses & Groundcovers

Grasses and Groundcovers

Single, Cluster, and Silhouettes

Single and Cluster Leaves and Leaf Silhouettes

Single and Cluster Leaves and Leaf Silhouettes

Single and Cluster Leaves and Leaf Silhouettes

98

Single and Cluster Leaves and Leaf Silhouettes

Single and Cluster Leaves and Leaf Silhouettes

Single and Cluster Leaves and Leaf Silhouettes

101

Single and Cluster Leaves and Leaf Silhouettes

Single and Cluster Leaves and Leaf Silhouettes

104

Single and Cluster Leaves and Leaf Silhouettes

Single and Cluster Leaves and Leaf Silhouettes

106

Single and Cluster Leaves and Leaf Silhouettes

Single and Cluster Leaves and Leaf Silhouettes

Single and Cluster Leaves and Leaf Silhouettes

Single and Cluster Leaves and Leaf Silhouettes

110

Single and Cluster Leaves and Leaf Silhouettes

Single and Cluster Leaves and Leaf Silhouettes